Civic Skills and Values

Teamwork

By Dalton Rains

www.littlebluehousebooks.com

Copyright © 2024 by Little Blue House, Mendota Heights, MN 55120. All rights reserved. No part of this book may be reproduced or utilized in any form or by any means without written permission from the publisher.

Little Blue House is distributed by North Star Editions:
sales@northstareditions.com | 888-417-0195

Produced for Little Blue House by Red Line Editorial.

Photographs ©: Shutterstock Images, cover, 4, 7, 8–9, 11, 15, 17, 18–19, 20, 23, 24 (top left), 24 (top right), 24 (bottom left), 24 (bottom right); iStockphoto, 12

Library of Congress Control Number: 2022919910

ISBN
978-1-64619-824-5 (hardcover)
978-1-64619-853-5 (paperback)
978-1-64619-909-9 (ebook pdf)
978-1-64619-882-5 (hosted ebook)

Printed in the United States of America
Mankato, MN
082023

About the Author

Dalton Rains writes and edits nonfiction children's books. He lives in Minnesota.

Table of Contents

Being a Helper **5**

Alone Time **13**

Why It Matters **21**

Glossary **24**

Index **24**

Being a Helper

Teamwork is about helping one another. Everyone does their part.

Teamwork happens
at school.
You help solve problems
in class.

Teamwork happens
with family.
You help your sister in
the garden.

You help your parents.

Everyone has a job.

You all help clean

your home.

Alone Time

Sometimes it is hard to be part of a team.
You might want to work alone.

You might feel tired.
Or you might feel angry
with others.
It is okay to be
alone sometimes.

But sometimes you have to be with others.

Then teamwork matters.

Try to listen to others.
Try to help when you
are able.

Why It Matters

Teamwork makes big jobs easier.

You work together to help clean up.

Teamwork means you help one another. When you work together, you can do anything.

Glossary

class

home

garden

tired

Index

C
clean, 10, 21

F
family, 8

J
jobs, 10, 21

S
school, 6